Kay Bell

CRY

SWEAT

BLEED

WRITE

LILY POETRY REVIEW BOOKS

Published by Lily Poetry Review Books
223 Winter Street
Whitman, MA 02382

https://lilypoetryreview.blog/

ISBN: 978-1-7337683-7-5

Cover Design: Naomie Jean-Pierre and Martha McCollough
Cover Art: Naomie Jean-Pierre

ACKNOWLEDGEMENTS

"Maybe" & "And" first appeared in *The Free Library of the Internet Void*
"Waiting for Morning" first appeared in the *Lily Poetry Review*
"Sisters" & "Harlem" first appeared in *Moko Caribbean Arts and Letters*
"Magic" first appeared in *K'in*

Table of Contents

CRY

SWEAT

BLEED

WRITE

CRY

I have an ocean of courage buried somewhere deep inside me.
I know this, because I taste the salt every time I cry.

-Tyler Knott Gregson

Maybe

Maybe, we all got on the flight to America;
our sister and I shared the window seat;
you sat on mummy's lap
and then she left us.
Maybe, you will have your first birthday in Apt 5A.
Cake, ice cream and our sister's cries
balanced on the rooftop of grandma's bad temper.
Then, we grow up sitting stone faced on top of the blue velvet sofa,
silent talking, believing *mum's coming back.*
We brave the brown leather straps; eat Dinty Moore beef stew,
and read stories about siblings who were abandoned
but still humane enough to leave bread for the birds.
I can see us all now, checks stamped to our foreheads,
overweight and voiceless;
Maybe we will love each other?
Subsequently, mum will return with war stories
by courtesy of her husband who proudly smashes her face against the seasons.
Then again, you can always pretend it never happened;
slip out of mummy's lap,
cry on the white beach of Barbados, pick up your packages from the Mail service,
eat Avocados out of your backyard
and write Christmas cards to the 17-year-old that birthed you.

The First Day of School

You never forget the first day of school
your mum holding your quaking hands,
and the plate size pancakes that made your stomach full.

You adjust your black polyester skirt,
its silver dime buttons against the side of a brand-new woman
and let your mum's hand go back to its place.

You walk in leather shoes, sliding against your ankles
and the itchy tights nailing the fresh silk of your thighs;
you wave goodbye without looking her in the face.

And then you meet your teacher, who could've been
your mum. Her hands sturdy and firm, take you to your seat
where you sit and forget the bruises on your darling mother's face.

And

& the person behind the counter is a man

& he reminds me of my father

& he is a gray haired, pretentious, bastard

& he is talking slow and careful

& somehow I have begun to romanticize our meeting

& take him in my closet to dream his shirt off

& he is mine

& we fall apart between spring and summer

& I begin again

& then the man says: "6 dollars and 50 cents"

& I look up

& my father is gone

& I recognize there's something about loving a man who's hurt you

Waiting for the Morning

The therapist asks: *how do you feel?*
& I feel authenticated
           because
someone wants to know   what it feels like
           to be a black woman who is afraid of the dark

& I keep telling myself to stop feeling   this way
           because my sons are watching
& there is no one else   no one else
           there is no one else

& now I am sitting on the bus
next to a man eating a bagel
& his shirt is torn   and he is calloused
& I'm thinking of holding his hand,   but he is leaving
& the sun is going down   & gravity becomes God
& God is humid and aching

& now the therapist is asking: *will you be here tomorrow?*
           & I just cry   incapable of explaining
how difficult it is   to anticipate the morning

Dreaming Us Alive

In this dream,
we aren't just roaming the streets,
our bodies are engraved in purpose:
portraits of black clouds   stretching across the sky,
& we are certain our steps have no limit.

I have waited a long time for you.

but something is happening that scares us,
        me.
Where we once believed in what's intimate,
we're now sponsored by aching.
        You've become intensely undefined.   I'm crazy,
these may be inaccurate emotions
but in my defense   I've never had a father
& this world has become warring rose petals
planting grief into a garden,
I visit   periodically.
        I find you   untamed   & wrong about everything.
I do not make a noise.   I attach my feet to the wind
        & gather my fear.
I've only been gone a day
        but I've learned so much.
Young girls aren't the only ones to get broken,
        poets break too.

SWEAT

Anything like flowers had long ago been drowned in the salty stream that had been pressed from her heart. Her tears, her sweat, her blood. She had brought love to the union and he had brought a longing after the flesh

– from Zora Neale Hurston's *"Sweat"*

Love & War

After Ocean Vuong

& I'm waiting to be rescued

because these stained hands
are empty   quivering
        full of war.

Waiting   where the thorns
      are buried
& rain bruises   the night.

Waiting

where the black wolf
wears   red lipstick

& everything beautiful
        is sealed   in a box.

Waiting because   my heart is a lullaby
        dubbed from   a hummingbird

& our love is splintered
      unfinished
&
    knifed to the wall.

Untitled 6

Sometimes you go into the deep

    of yourself and stay. No one

        can find you, in the busy lights and

            you go to where you are big. Some

                place you're used to. You go into

                    lacking; into the spaces that scare

                        me and tell me to stay away before

                            I sink or swim alongside of you.

                        You go and I stare from the living room,

                in awe of the madness. Afraid

            of the lights and the depth of

            your going. You go deep, deep

        where there is gray and yellow

    and where babies do not cry and

    where soundless beginnings come.

You go, and relish solitude.

Night

a wound inside a black man

his grief impregnating a black woman

his father gone

him craving for the taste of African soil

him returning suffocated in his strength

the feeling of his unhealing, breaking an entry inside his children

his body; the middle passage

him caged inside his labored breaths

him never learning his real name

his appetite for death

his mother calling him a sissy

him dissolving in a line-up

his hands born in a handcuffed womb

his manhood bricked into glass

his weeping in the closet

his laughter collapsing into concrete

his home incarcerated in a memory

his lips as a ballad of heartache

    the way I love him.

Library Song

Because you appear
as the books collapse,
and then,
stand at the table
stroking
the top layer of my womanhood,
and the frail points of every angle
I have formed,

I take you in,
biting your flesh 'til the ugly parts show.

You like it.

We read colored faces
without identities;
masculine versus feminine
and broken unions
swept away like dust.

My legs warn you.
I will not break here.

I fold you in my creases and save you for later.

What are we doing?
How did it come to this?

I'm tearing the pages from the books
and reading the stories in breaths.

Go home.

The light is on
and mahogany arms grab you,
carrying you
to where I can't reach.

Sisters

for Melissa

Two girls.

No pigtails,

or "what do you want to be when you grow up?" stories,

just grandma trembling,

with abandonment.

Two girls,

light/dark,

seasoned with dilemmas,

looking for love and pain, in New York City.

No pigtails,

grandma's tears.

Abandoned.

Trembling.

"What do you want to be when you grow up?"

Eve

after Alessandro Nesci's Portrait of a Girl

in man's deep sleep
she came
teaching us   to come quietly
to gather the meat of the rib
      between the rustle of leaves
      and geraniums

      to make something of it

to bear the burden of masculinity
while naked   and scattered

&
undone by romance
slithering
in the seam of her toes

      who was she?

the one who hungered for fruit?
the heritage of sin.

the evolution of bone from bone   flesh of flesh.

or is she simply

where I am too   just a fallen woman?

BLEED

In this part of the story I am the one who
dies, the only one, and I will die of love because I love you,
Because I love you, Love, in fire and blood

-Pablo Neruda

Bittersweet

Handsome outlines look for me in a world where I return each time the seasons change.

I love you,

Because these men, their hard-ons & cheap colognes desire the poem I'm writing, the hairs that fall off my shaven legs, and sometimes the rain that sleeps in me.

But I have tattooed you on my finger, as you fancy beauty I cannot comprehend; a variety of women who are all stuck in parking lots looking for love.

But because it will take all day to hate you, I stop, midday, to buckle the Steve Madden flats you bought after fucking someone else.

I will always love you

Untitled #14

I have spent so long
      covered in shame
      about the dead things
I know
buried at the bottom
      of my coffin feet.

Half the time I was
      spinning
in glass slippers
towards
      a cover up
      a mask
      a pack of cigarettes
      a calloused man
who had potential
but no mind to find it.

Sometimes,
the shame comes
over my bridged heart
where I'm nibbling   the oaths of pity.

But most times,
I'm a broken clock
useless &   filled to the brim
with minutes   of confusion.

& what if everything we ever knew was wrong?

What if my quarreling with peace
is the real reason
each word I write is dying
and each weeping sound
      turns out to be a threat.

I keep saying I know the reasons why you came
and I've acknowledged how you left,

but I know nothing about how you will die
or just how much you've changed me.

The Beauty of Broken...

I dare you to leave.

Un-hold my hand
and pack your regrets
in the black bag with yellow lining.

The kids will watch
and I will cry uncontrollably
in the corner
where the cup
of very black
and strong coffee
just barely missed your head.

Free me.

I am not yours.

This life is not ours.

I cannot compete
with the beauty of your secrets.

Take your toothbrush
and don't forget:
This is not a love thing.
This is not a revolution.
This is us.

Immolation

In night beauty,
   with red lips,
my aunt enters,
   with war secrets,
& her Joan of Arc smile.

She waits,
   until he lies again,
(until he is no longer human,
   & the stars stop coming,)

to begin screaming his name.
   He disappears into the black,
to slip his gold fingers
   around   silk hips.

He lines the equator with
       the flaming desperate bodies,

and then returns
   to burn the street.

My aunt screams.
       Ash
falling from her fingers.

& as her screaming stops,
   he takes her somewhere private.

They dance, make love
   & bury what's broken
in the impenetrable.

Harlem

Harlem
raised me
no milk
here,
the eighties
with drugs
and music
and grandma staying up
all night
to talk to silhouettes,
tall, dark and ugly.
Harlem fathered me
mothered my anxiety
and without loving arms
and afternoon snacks
Harlem took my innocence
and left me
homeschooled
and remote
fragile
but sturdier
than my past.
Harlem stood beside
all I didn't know
and got me familiar
with Avenue after Avenue
of relinquishment.
Smells of failure
and botched healings,
there were no recoveries,
no Brownstones,
no cream-colored faces,
only disjointed
colored dreams
dying with the music
and drugs

and abandoned babies
left to be taken care of
by grandmothers
who cried
missing their dark lovers/fighters
and misplaced daughters
who pierced the flesh
with white teeth
and ruined hands.

Write

Writing is utter solitude, the descent into the cold abyss of oneself.

-Franz Kafka

Work Sonnet

A man enters the office. I am the first person he sees

and the first person he walks past, to get to the white woman

sitting in the hall. The second person he will talk to when the

white woman explains he must see me for answers. As his feet

retreat towards my desk, a violence begins to stir. His apology

knifes resentment into my chest. He is the type of sorry that thinks

it was *too bad Trayvon was the unarmed one or GZ would be dead,*

the type of sorry that needs evidence from a black man that he is an

American, the type of sorry that thinks it's *women who are the n-word*

of the world, the type of sorry that says: *I thought he had a gun.* And

now I'm handing the man a stack of papers, telling him where to sign.

He thanks me without looking into my face. As he leaves the office,

he runs into a friend at the door. They chat, share a brief laugh and

then his friend walks towards the white woman sitting in the hall.

Magic
for Cynthia Cruz

You speak
        about things
                I know about,
stubborn doors of nakedness,
    feral,
              in the moonlight,
                            while unloading
        magical miniature
daydreams,
          onto Harlem doorsteps.
You speak
      & I hum,
                into myself,
a language
           I've never heard,
    a song
                that will not un-sing itself;
        a sort of lyrical madness,
                    in the space
                        where the homeless
        man and woman
              who were dead,
existed
          in a tiny silk box.
                        The murals paint your
wild blonde hair
      with poetic ceremonies;
                  tamed moments;
          bestial;
undomesticated;
        they cannot sweep you away.   And as you cradled your losses
& formed screaming walls

into mad speeches,
the magic of the feral
speak to me.
They provoke chaotic beginnings,
living where everything ends,
assembling my life;
so that I can once again
become myself.
It is now,
that I know,
there are some things in this world
that speak magic,   and like you,
those things are
exquisitely   uncultivated;   feral
and they   whisper a language   that shouldn't be tamed.

John 1:1

in the beginning the word was with God
the word   was God   &
now I'm afraid to say
the word that steals the morning before toast and eggs   before my mother calls
to say her word;   a word I refuse to pronounce.
Words that remind me
where this poem began
comingtogether;
Words forming something   I really don't want
Words that somehow sacrifice the person   needing them.
Words   that   cannot   be   beautiful.
Words that no one solicits.
in the middle of the night,   during a snow storm.
Words that have become desperate
Words that have h o l e s,
Words that cannot be trusted
Because who knows what these words do when they're alone?

Because who knows what these words do when they're alone?
Words that cannot be trusted
Words that have h o l e s,
Words that have become desperate
in the middle of the night,   during a snow storm.
Words that no one solicits.
Words   that   cannot   be   beautiful.
Words that somehow sacrifice the person   needing them.
Words forming something   I really don't want
comingtogether;
where this poem began
Words that remind me
to say her word;   a word I refuse to pronounce.
the word that steals the morning before toast and eggs   before my mother calls
now I'm afraid to say
the word   was God   &
in the beginning the word was with God

30

Untitled #15

turns out

the body keeps turning in a way the heart does not remember.

Sometimes scrambling on a path of half-forgotten bones

or speeding towards a hand feeding it what it hungers   but cannot bear.

Sometimes the body only has its feet
carrying it to places that feel like home,

where it spends the entire day   sitting in a chair
trying to remember,

what it used to trust in man's uprooting flesh.

Sometimes the body's on a journey down
an eternal street
in arms   that cannot hold it.

It kindles,

in its pleading to the heart,

sometimes jutted enough to forget its vacancy,

sometimes   humming the songs of disaster,

sometimes running its fingers over the thicket of hope,

sometimes trapped like a balloon caught in the palm of a child's hand,

sometimes witnessing the war that brings it closer to God,

sometimes   pivoting,

taking the heart   where it was never meant to go

turns out
sometimes the body is not the body

but what's left of what didn't explode…

.

Liberation

for Georgia O'Keefe's The Black Place

With this stone, I am no melancholy woman:

> relentless
> in consideration of death
> in the dark gray morning
>
> or groaning at the sunlight
> slipping between the rock.
>
> Instead,
> I become a voice   emerging
>
> from the borders of winter;
> a victor in the parting
> of the red sea
>
> a root thrived
> in the smallest part of earth
>
> whispering: here I am   here I am   here I am

> free

ABOUT THE AUTHOR

Kay Bell can be quoted: "If it makes me cry, sweat or bleed, then it is worth writing about." Her work appears in the book "Brown Molasses Sunday: An Anthology of Black Women Writers", The Lily Poetry Review, Moko: Caribbean Arts and Letters, The Write Launch, PRONG & PROSY and other venues. She earned an MFA at The City College of New York and lives in the Bronx. She considers herself a bibliophile.

CPSIA information can be obtained
at www.ICGtesting.com
Printed in the USA
BVHW051319130120
569380BV00013B/577/P